Beautiful Etudes

Artistic ... es
Technical D... Piano

Selected and Edited by **Vic... McArthur**

Alfred

Foreword

TO TEACHERS

Etudes have provided pianists with valuable technical training for generations. Today's pianists have more demands on their time than ever before, therefore, the materials chosen for study should be of the highest musical quality, worthy of the time expenditure. The pieces in *Beautiful Etudes* have been tested and chosen by piano students and teachers not only for their technical effectiveness, but also because they are lovely musical works.

UNIQUE FEATURES

- 14 artistic studies
- Arranged in progressive order of difficulty
- Written in accessible keys
- Difficult rhythms clarified

OTHER FEATURES

- Technical goals for each etude
- Composer biographical information
- Practice directions for each etude
- Suggested keys for transposition
- Creative suggestions for further musical and technical exploration
- Mastery and memorization checklists
- Glossary

SUGGESTIONS FOR TEACHERS

- Play each etude for the student. Modeling of expressive playing is essential to convey musical and technical ideals.
- Provide concrete practice steps for the student, including slow, hands-separate practice with a metronome.

with special thanks to Christine, Elisabeth, Lesley, Michelle and Sue

Table of Contents

NOTE: *Most titles are editorial.*

 **BEFORE YOU PLAY**

- On the closed key cover, block ("play" together) each broken chord with correct fingering. *Hint:* If the stretch is too large for your right hand, cross over and play the top note with the left hand.

- Circle the dynamic marks in measures 1–7 and measure 11.

 **AS YOU PLAY**

- Listen for a graceful melodic "shape," tapering off so that the last note of measures 1–6 is softer.

- Listen for seamless pedal changes, with no "thumps" or gaps in sound.

 **TRANSPOSE**

- *High Tide* is written in D minor.

- Transpose measures 1–6 to E minor. In E minor, which notes are sharp in measures 5–6?_____ _____

 **CREATE**

Change the rhythm to make the groups of eighth-note triplets sound "short-short-long."

Example:

etc.

short short long short short long

You might think of the "short-short-long" rhythm as:

etc.

PRACTICE RECORD

Date learned_____

Date memorized_____

 **omposer Facts**

Cornelius Gurlitt (1820–1901), German, was an organist, teacher and student of the composer Carl Reinecke (1824–1910). Best known as a composer, Gurlitt authored over 250 works, many of which continue to be played today.

High Tide

Op. 82, No. 80

Cornelius Gurlitt

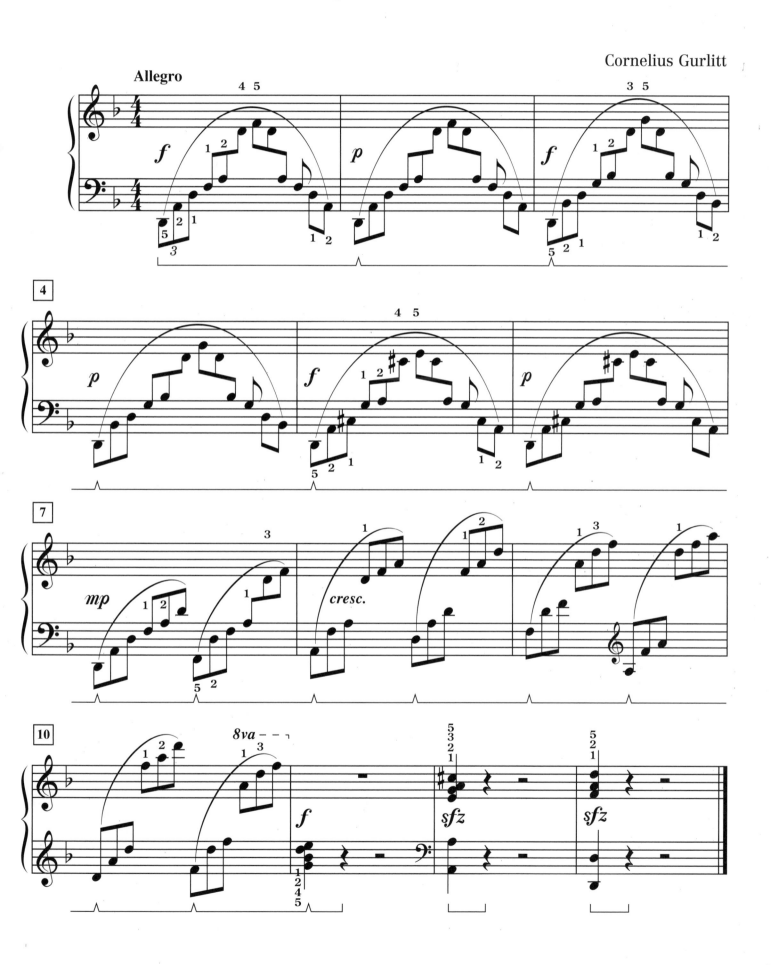

 **BEFORE YOU PLAY**

On the closed key cover, slowly "play" hands together. Try to imagine the sound and feel of the expressive dynamics. Especially notice how measures 3–4 echo measures 1–2, and measures 11–12 echo measures 9–10.

 **AS YOU PLAY**

Listen to the different phrase lengths as they change from two-measure phrases (measures 1–2, etc.) to four-measure phrases (measures 5–8, etc.).

 **TRANSPOSE**

• *Smooth Sailing* is written
  in _____ _____.

• Transpose measures 1–8 to C major.

 **CREATIVE**

Vary the RH melody in measures 1, 3, and 5–7 by using the same notes as written, but in a different order.

Example:

Composer Facts

Ferdinand Beyer (1803–1863), German, was best known for his arrangements of music originally written for orchestra and opera. He wrote a comprehensive piano method that is still used by teachers today.

Smooth Sailing

Op. 101, No. 75

Ferdinand Beyer

◦〜◦ BEFORE YOU PLAY

On the closed key cover, tap the rhythm hands together, counting aloud. Continue to "feel" the triplet rhythm during the quarter notes in measures 3–4 (and similar places).

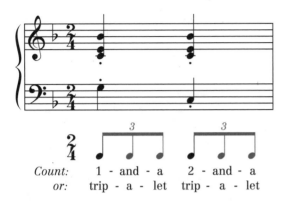

Count: 1 - and - a   2 - and - a
or: trip - a - let   trip - a - let

◦〜◦ AS YOU PLAY

- Listen to avoid playing the LH thumb too loudly in the scale passages. Instead, let the thumb "sneak" under the other fingers to play lightly.

- Be careful in measures 4, 8 and 12 to sustain (hold out) the RH half notes through beat 2.

◦〜◦ TRANSPOSE

- *Saturday Morning* is written in _____ _____.

- Transpose the LH of measures 1–4 to G major. *Hint:* The LH starts with the sixth note of the scale.

◦〜◦ CREATE

Start every descending scale in *Saturday Morning* at a different dynamic level, then either *crescendo* or *diminuendo* through the next measure.

Example:

etc.

PRACTICE RECORD

Date learned_____

Date memorized_____

Composer Facts

Ludvig Schytte (1848–1909), Danish, was a druggist before he began his music training at the age of 22. His teachers included the respected composers Niels Gade (1817–1890) and Franz Liszt (1811–1886). He taught at music conservatories in Berlin and Vienna where he composed mainly for piano.

Saturday Morning

Op. 108, No. 22

Ludvig Schytte

ᴥ BEFORE YOU PLAY

- On the closed key cover, "play" hands together as you count aloud. Notice the hand crossings.

- Count the sixteenth-note triplets:

trip - a - let trip - a - let *etc.*

ᴥ AS YOU PLAY

- Each cross-hand arpeggio should sound as though one hand plays it in a single sweeping motion. Avoid accents on the first note of each triplet, except on beat 1.

- Listen carefully to your pedaling. Not only does the pedal help connect the notes in the arpeggios and chords, but it also helps to play loudly, with a full, ringing tone.

ᴥ TRANSPOSE

- *Majestic Eagle* is written in _____ minor.

- Transpose the entire piece to A major, the parallel major of A minor. Each C becomes a _____.

ᴥ CREATE

Play descending (not ascending, as written) arpeggios in measures 1–2, 4–5, 7–8 and 10–11. Each arpeggio pattern should begin and end on the same note.

Example:

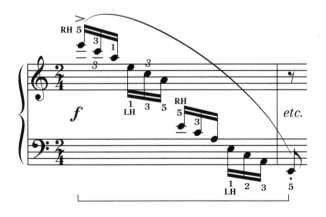

Composer Facts

(Paolo) Guiseppe (Gioacchino) Concone (1801–1861), Italian, was mainly known as a teacher of singing as well as a composer of vocal studies and other pieces for singers, including two operas. He also was an organist and choir master as well as a composer of piano studies.

PRACTICE RECORD

Date learned_____

Date memorized_____

Majestic Eagle

Op. 37, No. 2

Giuseppe Concone

BEFORE YOU PLAY

On the closed key cover, "play" the LH alone, being careful of all slurs and fingerings. Be aware of the shape of the melodic line.

AS YOU PLAY

- Play the LH alone. Listen for a "cello-like" sound as each note seamlessly blends into the next note within a phrase.

- Listen carefully to the RH. Do not underestimate its importance in propelling the piece forward with energy.

TRANSPOSE

- *Mystery Thriller* is written in _____ minor.

- Transpose the LH of measures 1–9 (beat 3) to A minor. Read the intervals carefully.

CREATE

Play both hands one octave higher, then one octave lower than written. Describe how the mood changes each time.

PRACTICE RECORD

Date learned_____

Date memorized_____

Composer Facts

Cornelius Gurlitt (1820–1901), *see page 4.*

Mystery Thriller

Op. 82, No. 65

Cornelius Gurlitt

BEFORE YOU PLAY

• On the closed key cover, tap the rhythm hands together.

• "Play" each hand separately on the closed key cover, being careful of the fingering.

AS YOU PLAY

• Listen to bring out the rhythmic motive (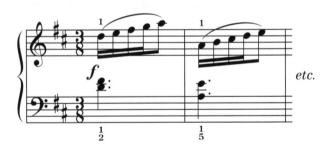) each time it appears.

• Listen carefully to connect the slurred notes in measures 33–40.

TRANSPOSE

• *The Brave Horseman* is written in ____ _____.

• Transpose the RH of measures 1–24 to D minor. Remember the B♭ and the raised seventh, C♯.

CREATE

Reverse the RH melody notes in measures 1–2, 5–6, 17–18, and 21–22.

Example:

etc.

PRACTICE RECORD

Date learned_____

Date memorized_____

Composer Facts

Cornelius Gurlitt (1820–1901), *see page 4.*

The Brave Horseman

Op. 130, No. 9

Cornelius Gurlitt

BEFORE YOU PLAY

On the closed key cover, "play" the RH of measures 3–6, then the LH of measures 19–23. At a fast tempo, the last note of each measure should be played with a gentle finger release rather than with a wrist release.

AS YOU PLAY

• Listen for a light *(leggiero),* crisp sound. For measures 19–26, the RH tone should become richer and should be played using more arm weight.

• Carefully pace the *poco rit.* in measures 25–26 before the *a tempo* at measure 27.

TRANSPOSE

• *Arabesque* is written in _____ minor.

• Transpose measures 50–55 to D minor. In D minor, which note is flat? _____

CREATE

• Make up words to fit the  rhythmic motive. Say them aloud as you practice.

• Play *Arabesque* softly and rather slowly. What is the mood now? _____

_____

PRACTICE RECORD

Date learned_____

Date memorized_____

Composer Facts

Johann Friedrich Burgmüller (1806–1874), German, wrote music that was quite popular in Paris society where his playing was also highly regarded. His melodic piano studies have been a significant part of the teaching repertoire since the time they were written, and are excellent preparation for the more difficult works of the Romantic Period.

Arabesque

Op. 100, No. 2

Johann Friedrich Burgmüller

Allegro scherzando

♋ BEFORE YOU PLAY

On the closed key cover, "play"
hands separately with special attention
to fingering.

♋ AS YOU PLAY

• Bring out the top note of each RH chord
  in measures 1–9 (beat 1) and 17–20.

• Play the LH legato in measures 1–8.

• There are several ways to "voice" (bring
  out) the melody in measures 9–16. One
  way is suggested below.

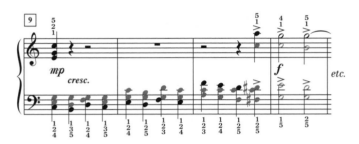

♋ TRANSPOSE

• *Choir Practice* is written
  in _____ _____.

• Transpose the LH of measures 9–16
  to D major.

♋ CREATE

Experiment with different melodic voicings
in *Choir Practice*. For example, play the
LH *forte* and the RH *piano* in measures 1–9
(beat 1). *Hint:* To "voice," slightly shift the
hand and arm so that more weight is used
on the note that you wish to make louder.

PRACTICE RECORD

Date learned_____

Date memorized_____

Composer Facts

Albert Biehl (1835–1899), German, was an
active composer of small salon pieces as well
as teaching pieces. Biehl was also well
known as a pianist during his lifetime.

Choir Practice

Op. 44, No. 6

Albert Biehl

BEFORE YOU PLAY

On the closed key cover, block ("play" together) each LH broken chord.

AS YOU PLAY

Stay loose (but not floppy) in the left forearm and wrist as you play. Listen so all the LH notes sound, yet remain a "murmur" under the RH melody.

TRANSPOSE

- *Busy Streets* is written in _____ minor.
- Transpose measures 1–8 to E major, the parallel major. Do the D♯ and G♯ change? _____

CREATE

Play the RH melody *legato*.
Does the mood change?

PRACTICE RECORD

Date learned_____

Date memorized_____

Composer Facts

Ludvig Schytte (1848–1909), *see page 8.*

Busy Streets

Op. 108, No. 8

Ludvig Schytte

✎ BEFORE YOU PLAY

- On the closed key cover, tap the rhythm hands together as you count aloud. Then, slowly "play" hands together.

- Study the key signature. Then, on the keyboard, play the A major scale. Play one octave, hands separately or hands together.

✎ AS YOU PLAY

- Listen carefully for crisp, even sixteenth notes. Play with curved fingers to achieve an exciting sound.

- Listen for the musical "surprises" in this piece (***p*** at measure 3, ***f*** at measure 5). At measure 9, start building the excitement until, at measure 13, the "fountain" bubbles over in celebration of the warmth of the sun.

✎ TRANSPOSE

- *Fountain in the Sun* is written in A major.

- Transpose measures 1–8 to G major, hands separately. The RH D♯s in measure 7 will become _____ ♯s.

✎ CREATE

Change the sixteenth-note rhythm patterns for an excellent technical workout:

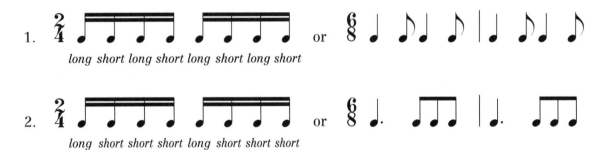

Composer Facts

Johann Wilhelm Hässler (1747–1822), German, was an organist, pianist, and teacher who knew C.P.E. Bach (1714–1788) and Wolfgang Amadeus Mozart (1756–1791). Almost all of his compositions were written for the keyboard.

PRACTICE RECORD

Date learned _____

Date memorized _____

Fountain in the Sun

Op. 38, No. 8

Johann Wilhelm Hässler

❧ BEFORE YOU PLAY

- On the closed key cover, block ("play" together) the RH broken chords in measures 49–62.

- This piece is built on a five-note melodic motive

(measures 1–2, etc.) that is transposed, varied and shifted from RH to LH. Locate and circle the first note of the motive each time it occurs throughout the piece.

- At measures 21–24, the motive appears in both hands. Why should the LH be emphasized (louder) there?

❧ AS YOU PLAY

In measures 49–62, keep the right wrist and forearm relaxed and level as you "rotate" to play the broken chords. Keep the thumb close to the key as you use small rocking motions of the right forearm instead of lifted fingers.

❧ TRANSPOSE

- *Rondo Militaire* is written in ____ _____.

- Transpose the LH of measures 1–8 (beat 1) to A major. Read the intervals carefully.

❧ CREATE

Imagine that *Rondo Militaire* is being played by a symphony orchestra. What instruments play at the beginning (measure 1)? _____

_____

At measure 33? _____

_____

At measure 49? _____

_____

PRACTICE RECORD

Date learned_____

Date memorized_____

Composer Facts

Ignace Joseph (Ignaz Josef) Pleyel (1757–1831), Austrian, lived in many places throughout Europe but finally settled in Paris, where he founded a music publishing business. His compositions were enormously popular during his lifetime, in part due to his ability to arrange and transcribe his own music.

Rondo Militaire

Ignace Joseph Pleyel

Allegretto moderato

❧ BEFORE YOU PLAY

- On the closed key cover, play the RH of measures 3–4 with a relaxed "fall" onto a firm (somewhat straight) 5th finger, followed by a gentle lift off the thumb.
- Play the LH in measures 17–23 with gentle "drop-lifts" for the slurs.

❧ AS YOU PLAY

Listen for all the dynamic differences in the A section (measures 1–16). In measure 9, the second sixteenth note should be *piano*.

❧ TRANSPOSE

- *Scherzo* is written in _____ minor.
- Transpose measures 1–8 to G minor. What are the flats in the key signature? _____ _____ What note is the raised seventh? _____

❧ CREATE

In measures 1–8, vary the LH chords to create a waltz-bass pattern.

Example:

PRACTICE RECORD

Date learned_____

Date memorized_____

Composer Facts

Carl Maria (Friedrich Ernst) von Weber (1786–1826), German, was renowned as a virtuoso pianist, composer, conductor and music critic. Weber was an influential force in German Romantic music, especially opera. His piano works sometimes exhibit elegant melodies and Classical-like passages, often demanding good scale and arpeggio technique.

Scherzo

Carl Maria von Weber

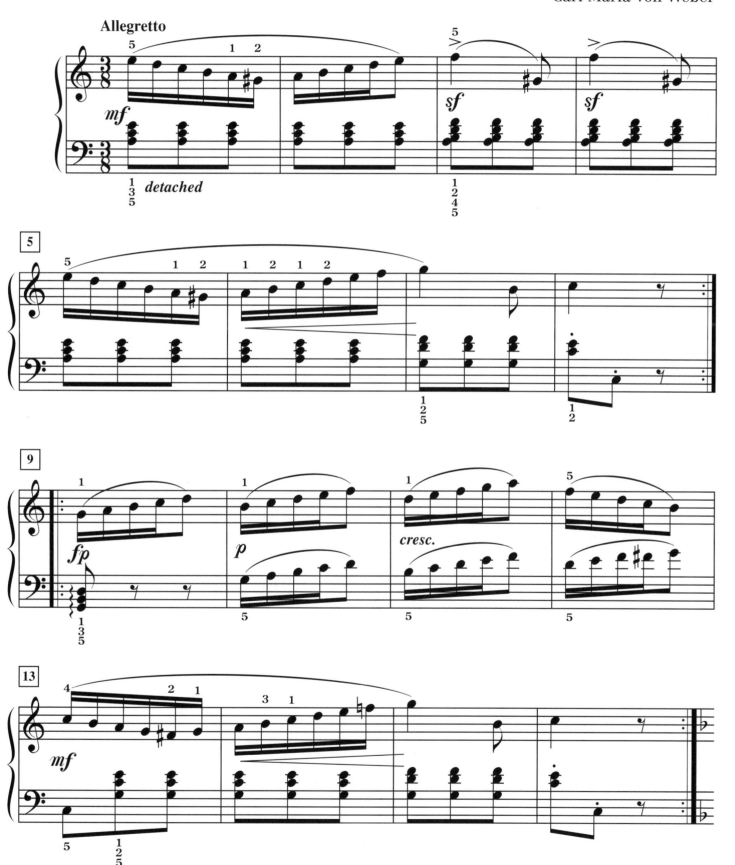

✿ BEFORE YOU PLAY

- On the closed key cover, "play" the RH alone with special attention to fingering.
- Look over the LH part, noticing especially the octave leaps in measures 9–13.

✿ AS YOU PLAY

- Play joyously, with a ringing, bold tone.
- Take time to physically prepare for the last chord, which should be played with a downward motion of forearms and hands.

✿ TRANSPOSE

- *Victory!* is written in B♭ major.
- Transpose the RH of measures 1–4 to C major.

✿ CREATE

Vary the LH intervals by playing them melodically ("broken").

Example:

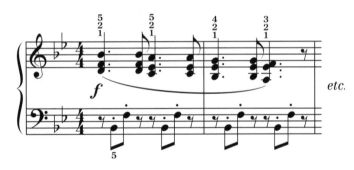

PRACTICE RECORD

Date learned_____

Date memorized_____

*C*omposer *Facts*

Ludvig Schytte (1848–1909), *see page 8.*

Victory!

Op. 108, No. 25

Ludvig Schytte

BEFORE YOU PLAY

On the closed key cover, tap both hands and count aloud. Take special care at measures 19–23 to observe rests, and at measures 53–56 to hold the notes for their full value.

AS YOU PLAY

- "Shape" the LH melody in measures 3–18 (and similar places) so that it is dramatic.
- At measure 31, let the single-note RH melody "sing out" sweetly over very soft LH chords.
- At measure 87 through the end, play with great feeling as the theme sounds a final time in both hands, then dies away. The last chord is a surprise ending.

TRANSPOSE

- *Ballade* is written in C minor (C major for measures 31–56).
- Transpose measures 1–10 to D minor. Think carefully about how the natural signs affect the notes when you transpose.

CREATIVE

A *ballade* (a French word, pronounced bah-LAHD), is a piece of narrative music that tells a story. Make up your own story for *Ballade*. How many characters are there? ____

PRACTICE RECORD

Date learned_____

Date memorized_____

Composer Facts

Johann Friedrich Burgmüller (1806–1874), *see page 17.*

Ballade

Op. 100, No. 15

Johann Friedrich Burgmüller

Glossary

TEMPO (from fastest to slowest)

allegro assai	very fast and lively
allegro con brio	fast and lively, with vigor and spirit
allegro scherzando	fast and lively, playful
animato	animated; fast and lively
energico	with energy
allegro non troppo	fast and lively, (but) not too much
moderato con moto	a moderate (medium) tempo, with motion
moderato deciso	a moderate (medium) tempo, definite and firm
andante maestoso	a walking tempo, majestic and noble
a tempo	return to the tempo, especially after *rit.* or *accel.*
tempo primo	return to the first tempo

DYNAMICS

accent (>)	play this note louder than those around it
forte-piano (fp)	loud, followed immediately by soft
pianissimo (pp)	very soft
sforzando (sf)	a sudden, strong accent (same as *sforzato*)
sforzato (sfz)	a sudden, strong accent (same as *sforzando*)

ARTICULATIONS

portato	halfway between *legato* and *staccato*; "long" *staccato*
tenuto (–)	hold the note(s) the full length; slight stress

OTHER

arabesque	a lyrical piece in an elaborate or embellished style
ballade	a piece that tells a story
cantando	singing (same as *cantabile*)
dolce	sweetly
grazioso	gracefully
leggiero (also *leggero*) (*legg.*)	lightly
misterioso	mysteriously
molto	much
octave sign (8va)	play an octave higher or lower than written
ped. simile	continue pedaling in similar fashion as previously marked
poco	little
risoluto	bold; with determination
scherzo	a musical joke; usually a fast, playful piece
tarantella	a fast Italian dance in $\frac{6}{8}$ meter; folk legend says that the dance supposedly could cure the bite of the tarantula spider